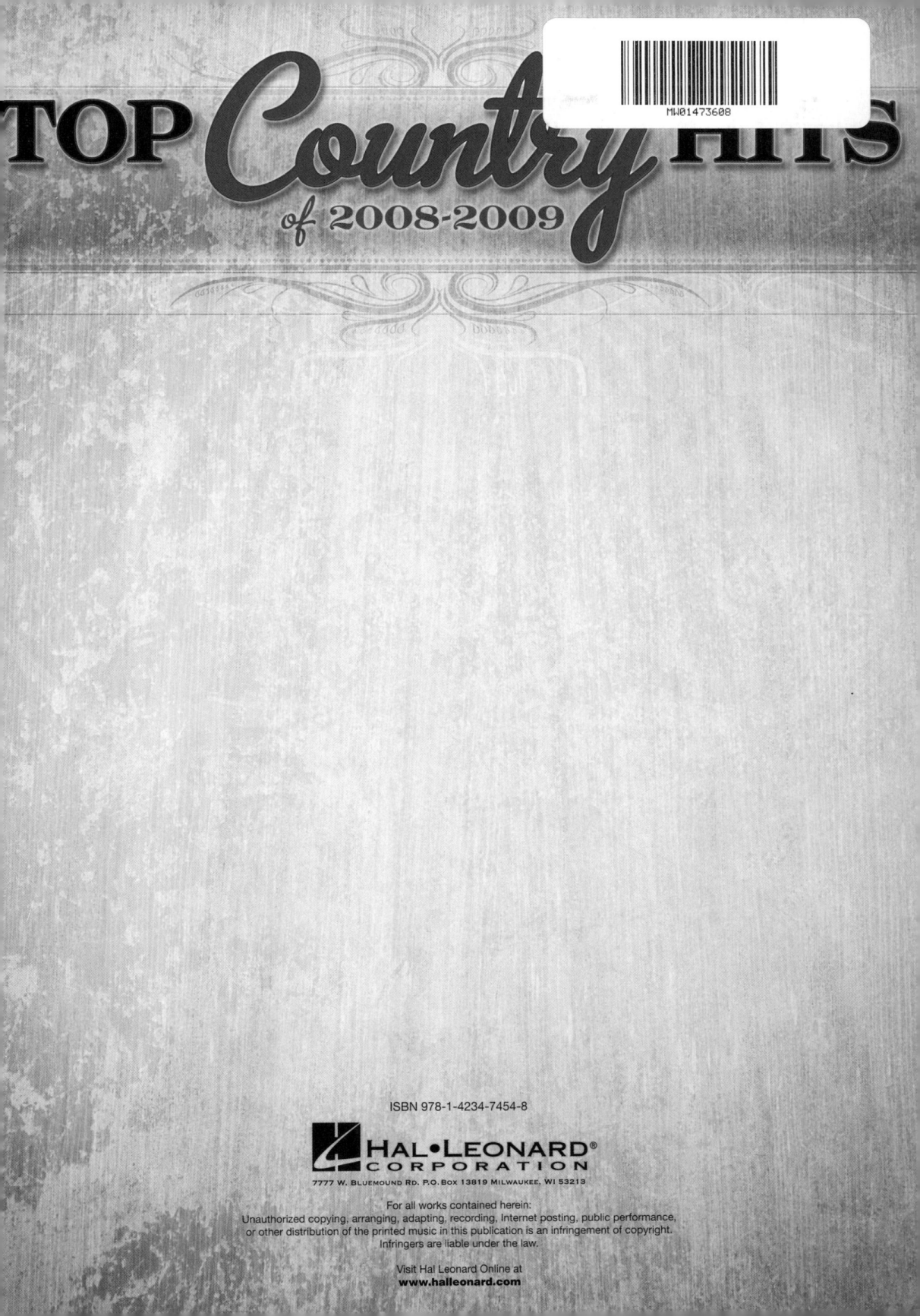

4	Already Gone	SUGARLAND
10	Change	TAYLOR SWIFT
16	Country Boy	ALAN JACKSON
24	Cowgirls Don't Cry	BROOKS & DUNN featuring REBA McENTIRE
31	Don't	BILLY CURRINGTON
38	Everybody Wants to Go to Heaven	KENNY CHESNEY
45	God Love Her	TOBY KEITH
52	Here	RASCAL FLATTS
60	Life in a Northern Town	SUGARLAND featuring LITTLE BIG TOWN & JAKE OWEN
66	Love Story	TAYLOR SWIFT
74	River of Love	GEORGE STRAIT
81	Roll with Me	MONTGOMERY GENTRY
88	Start a Band	BRAD PAISLEY duet with KEITH URBAN
97	Sweet Thing	KEITH URBAN
106	Waitin' on a Woman	BRAD PAISLEY
118	White Horse	TAYLOR SWIFT
112	You Look Good in My Shirt	KEITH URBAN

THE BEST EVER COLLECTION

ARRANGED FOR PIANO, VOICE AND GUITAR

150 of the Most Beautiful Songs Ever
150 ballads
00360735...$24.95

150 More of the Most Beautiful Songs Ever
150 songs
00311318...$24.95

Best Acoustic Rock Songs Ever
65 acoustic hits
00310984...$19.95

Best Big Band Songs Ever
68 big band hits
00359129...$16.95

Best Broadway Songs Ever
83 songs
00309155...$24.95

More of the Best Broadway Songs Ever
82 songs
00311501...$22.95

Best Children's Songs Ever
102 tunes
00310360 (Easy Piano)...$19.95

Best Christmas Songs Ever
69 holiday favorites
00359130...$19.95

Best Classic Rock Songs Ever
64 hits
00310800...$19.99

Best Classical Music Ever
86 classical favorites
00310674 (Piano Solo)..$19.95

Best Contemporary Christian Songs Ever
50 favorites
00310558...$19.95

Best Country Songs Ever
78 classic country hits
00359135...$19.95

Best Early Rock 'n' Roll Songs Ever
74 songs
00310816...$19.95

Best Easy Listening Songs Ever
75 mellow favorites
00359193...$19.95

Best Gospel Songs Ever
80 gospel songs
00310503...$19.95

Best Hymns Ever
118 hymns
00310774...$18.95

Best Jazz Standards Ever
77 jazz hits
00311641...$19.95

More of the Best Jazz Standards Ever
74 beloved jazz hits
00311023...$19.95

Best Latin Songs Ever
67 songs
00310355...$19.95

Best Love Songs Ever
65 favorite love songs
00359198...$19.95

Best Movie Songs Ever
74 songs
00310063...$19.95

Best Praise & Worship Songs Ever
80 all-time favorites
00311057...$19.95

More of the Best Praise & Worship Songs Ever
80 songs
00311800...$19.99

Best R&B Songs Ever
66 songs
00310184...$19.95

Best Rock Songs Ever
63 songs
00490424...$18.95

Best Songs Ever
72 must-own classics
00359224...$22.95

More of the Best Songs Ever
79 more favorites
00310437...$19.95

Best Soul Songs Ever
70 hits
00311427...$19.95

Best Standards Ever, Vol. 1 (A-L)
72 beautiful ballads
00359231...$17.95

More of the Best Standards Ever, Vol. 1 (A-L)
76 all-time favorites
00310813...$17.95

Best Standards Ever, Vol. 2 (M-Z)
72 songs
00359232...$17.95

More of the Best Standards Ever, Vol. 2 (M-Z)
75 stunning standards
00310814...$17.95

Best Torch Songs Ever
70 sad and sultry favorites
00311027...$19.95

Best TV Songs Ever
64 catchy theme songs
00311048...$17.95

Best Wedding Songs Ever
70 songs
00311096...$19.95

FOR MORE INFORMATION, SEE YOUR LOCAL MUSIC DEALER, OR WRITE TO:

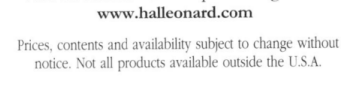 **HAL•LEONARD® CORPORATION**

7777 W. BLUEMOUND RD. P.O.BOX 13819 MILWAUKEE, WI 53213

Visit us on-line for complete songlists at www.halleonard.com

Prices, contents and availability subject to change without notice. Not all products available outside the U.S.A.

These great songbook/CD packs come with our standard arrangements for piano and voice with guitar chord frames plus a CD. The CD includes a full performance of each song, as well as a second track without the piano part so you can play "lead" with the band!

1. Movie Music
Come What May • My Heart Will Go On (Love Theme from *Titanic*) • The Rainbow Connection • and more.
00311072 P/V/G..$14.95

2. Jazz Ballads
Georgia on My Mind • In a Sentimental Mood • The Nearness of You • The Very Thought of You • When Sunny Gets Blue • and more.
00311073 P/V/G..$14.95

3. Timeless Pop
Ebony and Ivory • Every Breath You Take • From a Distance • I Write the Songs • In My Room • Let It Be • Oh, Pretty Woman • We've Only Just Begun.
00311074 P/V/G..$14.95

4. Broadway Classics
Ain't Misbehavin' • Cabaret • If I Were a Bell • Memory • Oklahoma • Some Enchanted Evening • The Sound of Music • You'll Never Walk Alone.
00311075 P/V/G..$14.95

5. Disney
Beauty and the Beast • Can You Feel the Love Tonight • A Whole New World • You'll Be in My Heart • You've Got a Friend in Me • and more.
00311076 P/V/G..$14.95

6. Country Standards
Blue Eyes Crying in the Rain • Crazy • King of the Road • Oh, Lonesome Me • Ring of Fire • Tennessee Waltz • You Are My Sunshine • Your Cheatin' Heart.
00311077 P/V/G..$14.95

7. Love Songs
Can't Help Falling in Love • Here, There and Everywhere • How Deep Is Your Love • Maybe I'm Amazed • You Are So Beautiful • and more.
00311078 P/V/G..$14.95

8. Classical Themes
Can Can • Habanera • Humoresque • In the Hall of the Mountain King • Minuet in G Major • Symphony No. 5 in C Minor, 1st Movement Excerpt • and more.
00311079 Piano Solo $14.95

9. Children's Songs
Do-Re-Mi • It's a Small World • Linus and Lucy • Sesame Street Theme • Sing • Winnie the Pooh • Won't You Be My Neighbor? • Yellow Submarine.
0311080 P/V/G $14.95

10. Wedding Classics
Air on the G String • Ave Maria • Bridal Chorus • Canon in D • Jesu, Joy of Man's Desiring • Ode to Joy • Trumpet Voluntary • Wedding March.
00311081 Piano Solo $14.95

11. Wedding Favorites
All I Ask of You • Don't Know Much • Endless Love • Grow Old with Me • In My Life • Longer • Wedding Processional • You and I.
00311097 P/V/G $14.95

12. Christmas Favorites
Blue Christmas • The Christmas Song • Do You Hear What I Hear • Here Comes Santa Claus • Merry Christmas, Darling • Silver Bells • and more.
00311137 P/V/G $15.95

13. Yuletide Favorites
Away in a Manger • Deck the Hall • The First Noel • Go, Tell It on the Mountain • Jingle Bells • Joy to the World • O Little Town of Bethlehem • and more.
00311138 P/V/G.......................................$14.95

14. Pop Ballads
Have I Told You Lately • I'll Be There for You • Rainy Days and Monday • She's Got a Way • Your Song • and more.
00311145 P/V/G.......................................$14.95

15. Favorite Standards
Call Me • The Girl from Ipanema • Moon River • My Way • Satin Doll • Smoke Gets in Your Eyes • Strangers in the Night • The Way You Look Tonight.
00311146 P/V/G.......................................$14.95

16. TV Classics
The Brady Bunch • Green Acres Theme • Happy Days • Johnny's Theme • Love Boat Theme • Mister Ed • The Munsters Theme • Where Everybody Knows Your Name.
00311147 P/V/G.......................................$14.95

17. Movie Favorites
Back to the Future • Theme from *E.T.* • Footloose • Somewhere in Time • Somewhere Out There • and more.
00311148 P/V/G.......................................$14.95

18. Jazz Standards
All the Things You Are • Bluesette • Easy Living • I'll Remember April • Isn't It Romantic? • Stella by Starlight • Tangerine • Yesterdays.
00311149 P/V/G.......................................$14.95

19. Contemporary Hits
Beautiful • Calling All Angels • Don't Know Why • If I Ain't Got You • 100 Years • This Love • A Thousand Miles • You Raise Me Up.
00311162 P/V/G.......................................$14.95

20. R&B Ballads
After the Love Has Gone • All in Love Is Fair • Hello • I'll Be There • Let's Stay Together • Midnight Train to Georgia • Tell It like It Is • Three Times a Lady.
00311163 P/V/G.......................................$14.95

21. Big Band
All or Nothing at All • Apple Honey • April in Paris • Cherokee • In the Mood • Opus One • Stardust • Stompin' at the Savoy.
00311164 P/V/G.......................................$14.95

22. Rock Classics
Against All Odds • Bennie and the Jets • Come Sail Away • Do It Again • Free Bird • Jump • Wanted Dead or Alive • We Are the Champions.
00311165 P/V/G.......................................$14.95

23. Worship Classics
Awesome God • Lord, Be Glorified • Lord, I Lift Your Name on High • Shine, Jesus, Shine • Step by Step • There Is a Redeemer • and more.
00311166 P/V/G.......................................$14.95

24. Les Misérables
Bring Him Home • Castle on a Cloud • Empty Chairs at Empty Tables • I Dreamed a Dream • A Little Fall of Rain • On My Own • and more.
00311169 P/V/G.......................................$14.95

25. The Sound of Music
Climb Ev'ry Mountain • Do-Re-Mi • Edelweiss • Maria • My Favorite Things • Sixteen Going on Seventeen • Something Good • The Sound of Music.
00311175 P/V/G.......................................$14.95

26. Andrew Lloyd Webber Favorites
All I Ask of You • Amigos Para Siempre • As If We Never Said Goodbye • Everything's Alright • Memory • No Matter What • Tell Me on a Sunday • You Must Love Me.
00311178 P/V/G.......................................$14.95

27. Andrew Lloyd Webber Greats
Don't Cry for Me Argentina • I Don't Know How to Love Him • The Phantom of the Opera • Whistle down the Wind • With One Look • and more.
00311179 P/V/G.......................................$14.95

28. Lennon & McCartney
Eleanor Rigby • Hey Jude • The Long and Winding Road • Love Me Do • Lucy in the Sky with Diamonds • Nowhere Man • Strawberry Fields Forever • Yesterday.
00311180 P/V/G.......................................$14.95

29. The Beach Boys
Barbara Ann • Be True to Your School • California Girls • Fun, Fun, Fun • Help Me Rhonda • I Get Around • Little Deuce Coupe • Wouldn't It Be Nice.
00311181 P/V/G.......................................$14.95

30. Elton John
Candle in the Wind • Crocodile Rock • Daniel • Goodbye Yellow Brick Road • I Guess That's Why They Call It the Blues • Levon • Your Song • and more.
00311182 P/V/G.......................................$14.95

31. Carpenters
(They Long to Be) Close to You • Only Yesterday • Rainy Days and Mondays • Top of the World • We've Only Just Begun • Yesterday Once More • and more.
00311183 P/V/G.......................................$14.95

32. Bacharach & David
Alfie • Do You Know the Way to San Jose • The Look of Love • Raindrops Keep Fallin' on My Head • What the World Needs Now Is Love • and more.
00311218 P/V/G.......................................$14.95

33. Peanuts™
Blue Charlie Brown • Charlie Brown Theme • The Great Pumpkin Waltz • Joe Cool • Linus and Lucy • Oh, Good Grief • Red Baron • You're in Love, Charlie Brown.
00311227 P/V/G.......................................$14.95

34 Charlie Brown Christmas
Christmas Is Coming • The Christmas Song • Christmas Time Is Here • Linus and Lucy • My Little Drum • O Tannenbaum • Skating • What Child Is This.
00311228 P/V/G.......................................$15.95